Law School Study Guides

Evidence MBE Outline

Green Ribbon Engagements, LLC

2015

Disclaimer:

Note from the editor:

Thank you for purchasing our Evidence MBE Outline. Enclosed, you will find a raw outline meant to save you time while studying for the Multistate Bar Examination (MBE). This outline covers the clear and concise definitions you will need to master in Evidence in order to be successful on the bar exam.

Best of on the Bar Exam and legal careers!

Evidence MBE Outline

I. IMPEACHMENT

- It is ALL about the witness that takes the stand (it can be about the defendant or the plaintiff but only if they take the stand).
- Impeachment is to see that the witness is telling the truth by asking what they said and what they did.
- Impeachment is generally always coming in because it goes to credibility.
- You can impeach your own witness.
- You can ask the witness that takes the stand about prior convictions and non-convictions.

  - **Convictions—Charged and Convicted**
    - **Honest/Truthfulness Crimes**
      - Always coming in/admissible
      - Examples: Money laundering, bribery, perjury, embezzlement, false pretenses, larceny by trick, Ponzi Schemes, identity theft, insurance fraud, fraud/misrepresentation, tax fraud, etc.
    - **Violent Felonies**

- ONLY admissible if:
    - 1. The crime was committed within the last 10 years AND
    - 2. It passes the judge's balancing test: The probative value of the evidence OUTWEIGHS its prejudicial effect.
- Examples: Rape, murder, burglary, robbery, battery, assault, kidnapping, larceny, etc.

- **Non-Convictions—Just accused**
    - **Honest/Truthfulness Crimes**
        - ONLY admissible if the attorney asking the witness is ONLY asking the witness. Cannot prove that the witness was accused of the crime through extrinsic evidence.
        - Examples: Money laundering, bribery, perjury, embezzlement, false pretenses, larceny by trick, Ponzi Schemes, identity theft,

insurance fraud,
fraud/misrepresentation, tax
fraud, etc.
- **Violent Felonies**
  - Never coming in!
  - Examples: Rape, murder,
    burglary, robbery, battery,
    assault, kidnapping, larceny,
    etc.

II. CHARACTER EVIDENCE
- It is about the defendant (and sometimes
  about the plaintiff that takes the stand in a civil
  case). It is NOT about the witness.
- Character evidence is to show prior bad acts
  of what the defendant did in the past to show
  that the defendant acted in conformity with
  doing something bad.
- Character evidence is generally inadmissible
  because the probative value of the evidence
  IS outweighed by its prejudicial effect.
- **Exceptions**

  - **Civil Case**
    - If the plaintiff or defendant's
      character is at issue, evidence of

their character can ONLY come in
in the following cases:
- 1. Defamation
- 2. Child Custody
- 3. Negligent Entrustment
- 4. Fraud/Misrepresentation

- **Criminal Cases (3)**
  - **1. Defendant Opens the Door**
    - When the defendant brings in a character witness to testify to the good character and good traits.
    - If the defendant at the bench opens the door by having a character witness come in and testify by taking the stand about the defendant's good character and good traits FIRST, then the prosecution can then bring in their own character witness to testify to the defendant's bad character and bad traits.
    - The character witness can only testify to the defendant's

truthfulness/honesty or peacefulness—and this will depend on the crime the defendant is charged with.

- If the defendant is charged with a dishonest/untruthfulness crime, then the character witness can only testify to the defendant's honesty and truthfulness.
- If the defendant is charged with a violent felony, then the character witness can only testify to the defendant's peacefulness.

- **2. Prosecution can bring in circumstantial evidence to show MIMIC**
  - This is not to show that the defendant committed the crime, but the reasons why he/she could or would commit the crime.
    - M—motive
    - I—intent
    - M—mistake
    - I—ID

- o C—common plan/scheme
  - ▪ **3. Habit (aka "routine practice")**
    - • The prosecution can bring in evidence of the defendant's habit/routine practice if this is how the defendant always acts this same way everyday.

III. SUBSEQUENT REMEDIAL MEASURES

- o Cannot enter evidence after an accident occurs to show that the defendant fixed something to prove negligence or liability.
- o After an accident occurs, a party is permitted to fix something to make it safe, and evidence of this is inadmissible to prove negligence or liability because it is contrary to public policy because we want to encourage people to fix things and make them safer.
- o However, it is admissible to introduce evidence to show that the item/product was within the person's ownership and control.

IV. OFFERS TO SETTLE/COMPROMISE

- o Cannot offer into evidence any statement made as an offer to settle a case to prove liability because it is contrary to public policy

because we want to encourage people to
settle their cases.
- o If an offer to settle a case is coupled with an
  admission both are INADMISSIBLE AND NOT
  SEVERABLE.
- o However, in order for this rule to apply, you
  need a dispute first.

V. OFFERS TO PAY MEDICAL EXPENSES
- o Cannot offer into evidence any statement
  made as an offer to pay medical bills to prove
  liability because it is contrary to public policy
  because we want to encourage people to pay
  for another's medical expenses if they caused
  them injury.
- o If an offer to pay medical expenses is coupled
  with an admission, then they are severable
  and ONLY the admission is admissible and
  the offer to pay medical expenses is
  INADMISSIBLE.

VI. JUDICIAL NOTICE
- o The judge/court may take judicial notice (i.e.,
  no additional evidence is needed) if the fact is
  one that is not subject to dispute or opinion to
  save the court time.

- Criminal Case
  - If the jury is instructed on judicial notice, the jury **MAY** accept the fact as a conclusive fact.

- Civil case
  - If the jury is instructed on judicial notice, the jury **MUST** accept the fact as a conclusive fact.

VII. BEST EVIDENCE RULE
- Generally, the original document must be admitted into evidence if the document is material to the case and you are testifying to the contents of the document.

- **1. What is the Best Evidence Rule?**
  - Always use the original document, and if you cannot get the original document, then a copy is okay as long as the copy is authenticated and there is no evidence of evidence tampering.
  - The presumption is that the copy is okay.

- o **2. When does the Best Evidence Rule apply?**
  - o When you are trying to prove that the contents of the document have legal significance (i.e., will, deed, employment contract).
  - o When you need the document to prove your testimony and there is no other way to prove your testimony other than the document.
    - ▪ **Exception:** If there is another way to prove what you are saying, then the best evidence rule will not apply.

- o **3. Completeness Rule**
  - o When one party is trying to admit only a part of a document, then the other party may require the entire document to be admitted so that nothing is taken out of context.

VIII. HEARSAY
- o Generally, hearsay is inadmissible.
- o Hearsay is someone's out of court statement to prove the truth of the matter asserted, and is generally not admissible.

- Exceptions

  - **1. Present Sense Impression**
    - Observations, like a reporter.
    - It is when the declarant (the person making the statement) is witnessing/observing the event and speaking about what they are witnessing/observing to someone else at the time the declarant is witnessing/observing the incident.

  - **2. Excited Utterance**
    - It is when the declarant is saying something while they are excited.
    - Look for screaming, shouting, yelling, bellowing, howling, etc.

  - **3. Then Existing State of Mind**
    - Emotions (love/hate) "I could never kill her, we love each other and were planning on going on our honeymoon."
    - Look for planning, intent, emotions.

- 4. **Business Record**
    - A document that is kept in the regular course of business—this means that this record is always maintained, updated everyday, etc.

- 5. **Dying Declaration**
    - 1. The declarant must believe that they are dying.
    - 2. The declarant must make a statement as to why they think they are dying.
    - 3. Only applies to homicide (murder/manslaughter) and civil cases.
    - 4. The declarant must be unavailable at the time of trial (i.e., they do not have to be dead, but they could be in a coma, lost, or plead the 5th Amendment).

- 6. **Statement Against Interest**
    - Declarant makes a statement that is against their own interest that tends to make them guilty or liable for something. A reasonable person would not make such a statement

and they are unavailable to testify at the time of trial.

- The declarant could be either a party or non-party (but it will typically be a non-party).
- The statement against interest will look like an admission, but it will not be an admission because it was made by a non-party typically.

- **7. Past Recollection Recorded v. Present Recollection Refreshed**

  - **Past Recollection Recorded**
    - Hearsay exception!!
    - The witness once knew about the document because generally the witness wrote it/adopted it/knows it, but currently cannot remember.
    - The attorney will present the document to the witness and the witness will verify if they wrote the document, and if they wrote the document, the witness will read it into evidence.

- The document will be read into evidence, where it will then become part of the record.

  - **Present Recollection Refreshed**
    - NOT hearsay.
    - The witness made something to remember the event, but has since forgot a fact.
    - The attorney will present the witness with a document to refresh their memory but this document will NOT be read into evidence.

IX. ADMISSIONS

- **1. Admission**
  - Always admissible.
  - Made by a party in a case, and also known as admissible as non-hearsay or admission of a party opponent.

- **2. Adoptive Admission**
  - When someone accuses someone else of doing something and the person who is accused of doing something bad stays

silent when they should have objected/refuted/denied the statement. This is an adoptive admission and is coming in against the person that stayed silent.
- However, if someone that accused someone of doing something bad was just making a joke, then the person that was accused of doing something bad will not have to deny/refute/object to the statement, and it will not be considered an adoptive admission.

- **3. Vicarious Admission**
  - When an employee makes an admission while working within the scope of employment that will be admissible and come in against the employer.

- **4. Prior Sworn Inconsistent Statement**
  - When an attorney brings in a party's prior sworn statement (i.e., a statement made under oath and subject to cross examination) (i.e., deposition, hearing, trial, etc.) and now the statement contradicts with the party's current statement.

- **5. Prior Consistent Statement**
  - When an attorney brings in a party's prior statement to show that it contradicts with the party's current statement, the party that is accused of making inconsistent statement can prove that the statement they said previously IS consistent with their current statement by refuting or denying the accusation.

X. PRIVILEGES

- **1. Attorney-Client**
  - 1. There must be a relationship between the attorney and client.
  - 2. Any communications made between the client and anyone providing legal services or professional services on behalf of the attorney is also protected by the privilege.
  - 3. The attorney and client must have communications made in a place that is confidential or where both attorney and client have a reasonable expectation of privacy.
  - 4. The attorney client privilege will still be effective even after divorce.

- Exceptions:
    - 1. If the client asks the attorney how to commit future crimes, then this will not be protected by the attorney-client privilege.
    - 2. If there is any type of dispute between the attorney and client, this will not be protected by the attorney-client privilege (look for fee disputes or malpractice disputes).

- **2. Doctor-Patient**
    - 1. Covers conversations related to medical treatment or diagnosis as to why the patient is being medically treated in the first place.
    - 2. The doctor patient privilege will cover all communications made between people who are there on behalf of the patient or for the interests of the patient (i.e., mom, dad, siblings, nurses, spouses, etc.).

    - Exceptions:
        - 1. If there is any type of dispute between the doctor and patient, this will not be protected by the doctor

patient privilege (look for fee disputes or malpractice disputes).
- 2. If the patient puts their condition at issue for others to hear, then this will also not be protected by the doctor-patient privilege.

- **3. Spousal Communication**
  - 1. This privilege applies to all cases.
  - 2. Privilege protects those confidential communications the spouses made to each other while married.
  - 3. This privilege will protect those confidential communications to spouses made to each other while married and this will survive divorce.
  - 4. If one spouse refuses to disclose information then, that spouse can stop the other spouse from disclosing information.
  - 5. Both spouses must jointly waive the privilege.

  - **Exceptions**
    - 1. The privilege will not protect child abuse or spousal abuse.

- 2. The privilege will not protect communications about joint crimes the spouses will commit.

- **4. Spousal Testimony**
  - 1. Only applies to criminal cases.
  - 2. The privilege will only apply if the spouses are married at the time of trial.
  - 3. The privilege will protect those confidential communications the spouses made to each other before and during marriage.
  - 4. When the spouses divorce, then the privilege ceases.
  - 5. Only the witness spouse holds the privilege and can choose to testify or not to testify against the defendant spouse— and there is nothing the defendant spouse can do to stop the witness spouse from testifying.

  - **Exceptions**
    - 1. The privilege will not protect child abuse or spousal abuse.
    - 2. The privilege will not protect communications about joint crimes the spouses will commit.

XI. WITNESSES

- **1. Lay Witnesses—Regular people**
    - 1. Any one can be a witness and testify so long as they have personal knowledge and a perception about something.
    - 2. A child can testify as a witness, so long as the child knows the difference between a truth and a lie.
    - 3. In federal court, a judge or juror cannot be a witness and testify in a case. BUT in state court, a judge and/or juror can be a witness and testify in a case.
    - 4. A witness can testify so long as they take an oath or affirmation to ensure that they will testify truthfully.

- **2. Expert Witnesses**
    - 1. To be classified as an expert witness, the attorney must lay a foundation, which means that the attorney must qualify the expert witness as an expert by showing the expert witness's CV, education, advanced education, background, training, work experience, publications, etc.

- o 2. Expert witnesses can only testify to the narrow issues they are actually and expert for.
- o 3. Expert witnesses can give an opinion and/or given an opinion of a conclusion in a case.
- o 4. However, an expert witness cannot testify about (i.e., give a conclusion) in a criminal case as it relates to the mental state of the defendant as it relates to an element of the case.

XII. AUTHENTICATION
- o To authenticate a piece of evidence, one party must use other evidence to support a finding that the evidence is what it claims to be or the evidence is what it purports to be.
- o 2. Types of evidence that needs to be authenticated:
  - o 1. Writings
  - o 2. X-rays
  - o 3. Pictures
  - o 4. Voice recordings
  - o 5. Objects
  - o 6. Maps and charts

- 3. Someone testifying to the document with personal knowledge is the most important part of authentication.
- 4. If you are trying to introduce an official or public document (i.e., a newspaper, notarized document, notarized contract, recorded deed, etc.) it does NOT need to be authenticated because it is already self-authenticated. This means that you do not need someone to testify to the document with personal knowledge because it is already authenticated.